1st edition: 06/2017

Author: ©Anne Reimerdes
Photos: Anne Reimerdes a.o.
Pictures authorized by artists

Anne Reimerdes - Rottberg 1 - 24402 Esgrus - Germany
Printed by: CreateSpace
in Germany by Amazon Distribution GmbH, Leipzig

For those who look around

the world is full of wonders,

although there are many more

which we cannot see.


To me

this is all the more reason

to make a poem

at least for what we can see.

# Table of contents

## Between the elements

Solid ground for feet to stand
means a really good foundation
for adventures on firm land,
approaching flood, though, irritation.

Torn between the elements
of earth with stones or the big sea
the dog possibly now repents
walking out so far and free.

A life in liberty contains
many decisions which might lead
often along conflicting lanes.
So weigh your chances and don't speed.

# When you see a face

What you see reveals a lot
about your own emotion.
Psychologists expertly spot
phobia or devotion.

From this angle you might see
a face, a skull, a back
of a body that does knee
and bend over some stack.

When you yearn to use your fingers
and turn the figure round,
you explore what else here lingers,
wakes phantasies unbound.

But be sure, you're not alone,
when you simply see a stone.

## Symmetry

We can be sure: before we once detected
any symmetrical proportion
nature came first and already perfected
such splendid forms without regret or caution.

Mathematicians are still proud of finding
the rules for symmetry in different forms,
which till today are generally binding
and for the artist represent accepted norms.

Our eyes are pleased when they see distinct beauty,
however, tastes do differ quite a lot.
Our culture makes us think it is a duty
to put each structure in its proper spot.

## Symbols

Mankind invented symbols just
to cut a message down and short.
For the recipient it must
give instantaneous report.

Common knowledge is expected,
otherwise misunderstanding
spoils the message thus infected
and endangers where it's ending.

Short messages in our days
use an emoticon or letter.
And you must know the role it plays
in understanding even better.

An extensive talk between
two or more is seldom seen.

## Slack line

It is not slack at all, the line,
but clearly it gives way
when you step on it, which is fine
when you stand firm, not sway.

Your sense of balance is at stake,
no easy feat of skill,
but for your own sweet ego's sake
you show courage and will.

The calmer you begin to walk
the steadier the line,
and when you concentrate, not talk,
your progress makes you shine.

5

# Joints

The stiff construction of the bone
keeps us erect when standing.
But with this rigidness alone
a fall would be tough landing.

So here come joints into the play
to link the bones in places
that are useful, too, to stay
or sit or move in cases.

Thus joints enable any motion
starting in our head,
which obeys some finer notion
of where we stop or tread.

### High and dry

Not much use are the watering cans
when they hang high and dry.
But they might serve some different plans
whose purpose can be wry.

A sense of humour clearly shows
in this odd decoration.
And the shrewd  visitor soon knows
this is an invitation.

So visitors are not hung dry,
but always welcome here,
they may go busy and learn why
watering cans are dear.

# The proper order

Sometimes to establish proper order
you simply turn things upside down.
Here someone took the wall as border,
painted it blue, the door just brown.

Everybody has their own
sense of order, as we know.
What to some seems wildly thrown
is for others right just so.

In our heads, what's right and proper
differs, too, with due respect.
The brains don't have a moral stopper
to right simply from wrong detect.

This decision is left free.
But what you do shows who you'll be.

## Want not - waste not

If you take care on what you lie
a mattress is the key.
When it is rotten, don't be shy,
insist on quality.

You want the comfort to sleep well
because you need the rest.
In the morning you can tell
which mattress was the best.

Your body thanks you, it's no waste,
to sleep well a no-brainer.
But here someone disposed in haste
his mat in the container.

## Open for greens

Open your eyes for our green
that is the basis of our life!
It may lose leaves, as can be seen,
politically cause of strife.

But nature doesn't think of waste,
recycling is no man-made thing
which has to be cleaned up in haste,
but takes its time developing.

The circle of a year goes by
and sometimes more before you see
from rotten greens that simply lie
new growth of life that's glad to be.

## Not straight

Who says a chimney must be straight
has never seen one quite like this.
So sometimes you will have to wait
for differences that you miss.

To some surprise is like a shock
because they need security
and regulations round the clock
to manifest maturity.

Others with a childlike mind
are open to spontaneous changes,
thus endeavouring to find
what mostly as "unusual" ranges.

## Shadow patterns

Contrasting patterns on the ground
strike the eye as a rare treasure:
We see in harmony with round
even square pavement is a pleasure.

And then we notice, quite surprising,
that shadows thrown without a thought
have a life as if advising
to look closer or see naught.

A mirror image drawn by shadows
moves along and changes form,
clear on streets, fuzzy on meadows
when the sun fights with a storm.

# Bed and breakfast

Taken apart the bed presents
high at the ceiling a fine view,
but unfortunately it prevents
from sleeping in it, tough luck, too.

But then, of course, the beds today
are bigger than those that were old.
When taller people want to stay
they like their feet not to be cold.

Today the mattress market makes
a religion of their brands,
when surely you would know it takes
mainly your money off your hands.

A sleep relaxing for your mind
should de-stress your body, too.
And after breakfast you unwind
and start the day as good as new.

# Flying like a bird

The sport of gliding takes a lot of patience.
The first part: to wait in a queue,
which leaves no room for any reclamations,
it simply is the pilots' equal due.

Keeping the balance stresses nerves for the duration
of being pulled along the runway when you roll.
But once you glide without a limitation
your sense of freedom gives you back what patience stole.

You glide in thermal spirals and enjoy
the feeling of a sailing bird of prey.
Down on the earth you leave things that annoy
and just forget what other people say.

You focus on the panel and keep checking
how high you fly and if the wings are stable,
make sure you have the other gliders' tracking,
but give and take "elation" is the label.

# The eye in the sky

Norbert Rath

It is not Google who does watch us here
but an eye far bigger than we know.
We can't escape this one so we stay clear
of things that hurt even before we go.

The eye called conscience is so hard to please
because it defies any concrete grip.
It is ingrained in us like a disease,
ever so often wielded like a whip.

Who made us think of what is right or wrong?
Did we come by it just by chance or how?
Where our primal ancestors so strong
that there's a guideline for us even now?

15

## In the limelight

No artificial light must shine
where nature shows its splendour.
The morning sunrays do just fine,
a thank you to the sender!

Exposed in limelight you stand bare
for people to admire
your looks or when loudspeakers blare
to focus on desire.

The crowd sees what they want to see,
which might completely differ
from what you really long to be,
not like this poppy, stiffer.

When transparent to all around
hard covers would allow
to save the centre you have found
before you have to bow.

## That's what roots are for

One purpose for roots is to hold on to their ground
so the tree does not fall over lightly.
They spread out to the side where the balance is found,
seldom seen like here so brightly.

For people the balancing act is to find
the roots that made their ways
into character traits, and not to be blind
for whatever inherent stays.

Accepting your roots means to let them hold
a major part of your being,
but your own life needs you to be bold,
be the person that people are seeing.

## No way out

There are moments in life when you see no way out,
you can *look* through a fence but not farther.
But as your heart still beats strong and stout
you would want to *do* something rather.

Then you let your mind wander around this fence
to discover the hole in the wall,
the one chance that maybe doesn't make sense
because it seems simply too small.

You take it and move on with baby steps first
and find the way out with new hope.
Then finally all the restrictions just burst,
and you laugh as you know you can cope.

## A hole in the ice

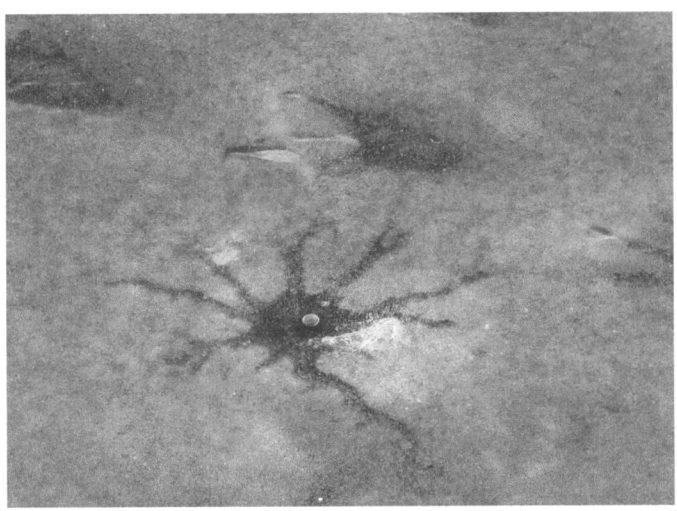

Two rivals with a stubborn mind
may ooze an icy charm,
and what they do best is to find
fault that produces harm.

The easy way is to go on,
stack coat on coat of ice,
so that the barricade you don
prevents from being nice.

It takes some force to break the ice
and find a smaller hole,
shaking your own pride is the price
by which you save your soul.

## Almost full

The moon is almost full, we say,
although, of course, that's wrong.
It is complete as well it may,
and always going strong.

Romantically touched we dream
in moonlight, full or not,
and thank the moon's silvery beam
for covering a blot.

A realist knows that the moon
keeps our earth in spin;
without it we would notice soon
the trouble we are in.

## Sun or moon

**Norbert Rath**

Could there be the moon so small
above the sun that's sinking,
hardly seen as a white ball
in unimportance shrinking?

Whereas the sun still lights the sky,
conjures colours, pastel shades
which all description would defy
in patches, stripes, bordering braids.

In no time this view dissolves
into darker colours till
you see the moon slowly evolves
and all the world is going still.

## Where the sun shines

Where the sun shines we call it 'day'
in either hemisphere,
though in the north it's hard to say
when winter days come near.

The darker such a day crawls past
the more depressed you're found,
and beg that winter does not last
much longer that year round.

Polar light does not boost emotion,
although it's such a sight
and gives you in the night a notion
of sun power so bright.

When the sun shines we like to live
and enjoy what it can give.

# The interruption of blue

**Norbert Rath**

The eye is pleased with such a sight
when blue shades alternate.
But on a sailing boat it might
bore when the winds abate.

A consequence of fickle wind
will be to pull down sails
whereby your sailing plans rescind
until more wind prevails.

Or looking closer you detect
a harbour straight ahead
So it is easy to deflect
from sailing then instead.

For then, the boat docked at the pier,
you can enjoy your can of beer.

23

# Deep waters

**Norbert Rath**

When you look across the plane of the sea
you can't see where there are shallow stretches.
So sea charts are meant a help to be
the guidelines that the sonar etches.

As paradoxical as it might sound:
the danger lies not in the deep
but where the shallow sands are found,
or stones near the surface sleep.

Deep waters run still with the currents below
which are normally hidden, but eventually show.

# Wide wild sea

**Norbert Rath**

When the weather gets rough and a bitter storm blows
unimpeded across the wide sea,
you experience moments when nobody knows
where the beginning or end of the sky used to be.

The waves reach at the sky and tower
above deep holes where boats can sink
and where the water shows its power
and can destroy you in a wink.

By tossing and turning the sea whips up spume
and the spray is blown in the air.
Stuck in this whirlwind you are right to assume
that the balance of power is not at all fair.

# Yellow sky

**Norbert Rath**

Like a long bowl of glass
the sky bears down on open seas.
The sun with its glaring yellow mass
hovers above, untouched by the breeze.

The sky is open and forever wide,
no ocean can with its expanse compete.
And we can never see the other side,
as restricted as our view must be.

We feel the sky above far or low,
close to the touch when clouds disperse.
But then the distance of stars does show
the unbelievable universe.

# Sailing into the night

Norbert Rath

The wind of the day has finally stilled,
orange skies promise calm weather,
some clouds that have been left to build
are at the end of their tether.

But now the sailor's skill is asked
when the trip in the dark is risked.
With luck the sea is moonlight basked,
bad - if away it's whisked.

Then you hope that the other sailors know
to put up their lights as you do.
You rely on equipment to trustworthy show
where to go when the plotter is new.

## Blue competition

**Norbert Rath**

Sometimes the sea looks calm and plane
and no waves toss water up and down,
the winds stalled and for once refrain
from roughing up the surface like a clown.

Movement in the sky comes to a halt,
the old waves turn into just tiny ripples,
the whipped up air still smells like salt
and the sharpness of our senses triples.

We hear, we smell, we see stagnation,
motion has slowed for the three boats
which almost seem imagination
that flies on air although it floats.

## Colours in the sand

Big stones with time to sand are ground,
lose colour as they crumble.
But after a close look around
you find colours to stumble.

Some grass or leaves in autumn red
can liven up the scene,
and the sandy ground instead
of grey seems partly green.

And take a handful of the stuff
that is called sand to see
the many tiny crystals gruff
or round in colours' glee.

# The epitome of soft

So soft that when you touch it it dissolves
in thousand tiny flakes of wool that fly.
On any surface that the wool involves
the flakes like a smooth cotton blanket lie.

Ephemeral and trembling to the touch
the seeds keep to themselves in a firm bond.
As if they knew it doesn't take as much
as a slight breeze to which they must respond.

That is the fate of softness that it stands
to lose whenever it is only slightly shoved.
And even carefully soft helping hands
would still destroy however well it's loved.

# Like tear drops

Like tear drops water assembles on the leaf
and stays until they almost burst.
Tears trickle down the face in silent grief
after they wet the blinking eyes at first.

The surface of the leaf, however,
repels the water so that it stays dry.
When engineers found this extremely clever
they thought this technically was the latest cry.

Nano particles keep water off the leaves,
so why not use them as a water shield?
But now we know the problem that this leaves,
which is a largely unexplored new field.

These particles are held back by no barrier,
in our body they pass each membrane,
which makes extensive use of them the scarier
the more they are employed. This is insane!

## Stand up

Stand up for yourself, don't stand someone else up,
or else no one wants to rely
on your promises, nor at one time look up
to you, however you try.

Stand up to hardship that turns down your way
and face it, for you are strong.
Although, of course, later you might have to say
that some decisions were wrong.

The question is whether you look at your face
in the mirror and do not resign.
You always live here and now in your place,
and can say "any error was mine".

# Farewell

**Norbert Rath**

A farewell often means a sad emotion,
you leave a person, a job or a place.
Disruption is final with your locomotion,
and sometimes you don't know what you have to face.

Although looking back can also show beauty,
some picture that you never want to forget.
But maybe you leave an escapable duty
so farewell becomes an agreeable set.

But sometimes a later return lies in store,
so you can enjoy every minute you stay,
because you are sure you will come here once more
and are welcome another farewell to say.

## Dog tired

A dog must sleep when it is tired.
Nothing helps but to lie down.
This is the way nature is wired
in contrast to each bigger town.

There life is pulsating around the clock,
sleep catches up only far between,
that it almost seems it has run out of stock,
there is always something that has to be seen.

An occasional nap, however, is healthy.
Nature simply insists on a break.
What good does it do if people are wealthy
but forget to sleep for their own sake.

## Just curious

When disasters have happened at places
lookers-on are normally curious.
But drawn to the site to see trouble on faces
their empathy is only spurious.

They cannot resist to slow their motion
and stop to see what's going on.
Like with journalists it seems devotion
to big sensations cries "come on".

They do not really care who needs
more than public interest.
But the hand that helps and feeds
consolation would be best.

The motivation for this zest to look
might lie deep in people's fear
that by a hair's breadth fate now took
someone else, but it came near.

## First and last

The first leaves are out and use the sun
whose warmth can finally set free
the structures that long have begun
to form in buds, not yet to see.

Last autumn days are known to start
the wonder that gives life anew
in buds carefully packed, apart
from everything winter can do.

So every spring we can enjoy
the spiral of updated life
which nature offers as a ploy
to conquer winter with its strife.

## September clouds

Waiting for the rain to drown
trees and fields in waterspout
I look rather up than down
and know what those clouds are about.

A sudden thunderstorm might blow
the wind hard in reverse direction
and thereby obviously show
unpredicted predilection.

Better for us to find a room
with walls around and a firm roof,
so that the clouds that above loom
can't harm us 'cause we're weatherproof.

## Autumn leaves leaves

Autumn leaves leaves to do what they must,
and that is to lose their green.
But this does not at all mean they go bust,
they simply know how to wean.

The tree saves its energy step by step
and reduces the danger to freeze.
And secretly it stays full of pep
until springtime sets out to tease.

When the temperatures rise the tree shows what it did
in the nondescript buds in the dark.
It slowly unfolds new leaves which get rid
of their covers as brown as the bark.

**From here on out**

Good intentions show remarkable patience,
they can wait for years to be carried out.
There are always reasons to have reservations,
for you can't be sure what things are about.

How easy life seems to be for the trees!
When they set out to grow they simply start.
There's no procrastination or wait for decrees
or the right point of time that would be smart.

Nature just tells them what happens and how,
whereas people plan and decide to take action
either tomorrow or next year or now
when there is surely no further distraction.

# Lifting the fog

A warmer day is rolled up to its end,
and from a lake fine drops of mist are lifted.
Until the morning molecules can send
dense water to be high up shifted.

The morning air smells fresh from dew,
you want to breathe in really deep.
And from afar as if on cue
you hear the early birds' clear peep.

A summer morning and its night
are a special pure delight.
Colours are dimmed and not yet bright
and you inhale the calming sight.

## Colourful petals

Colourful petals embrace the secret core
to a) protect and b) lure insects on.
The brighter and it also seems the more
they merrily the pollinators con.

Sometimes the irresistible attraction
is augmented by inviting smells
whose flavour can suffice in a small fraction
to reach a brain far faster than it tells.

So this is why we let the flowers speak
to silently convey a heartfelt message
and reach an aim which we secretly seek,
and hereby just facilitate the passage.

41

## Cherry trees

What use would be the cherry trees
if without help from early bees?
We'd see it blossom white in spring
but without bees no cherries bring.

And then an early frost can keep
the insects in their beehives deep,
when all temptation of the bloom
is prematurely cursed with doom.

So let us hope the climate change
won't the bees' timetable derange,
because what would we eat instead
if not the fruit in their bright red?

## Red and green

Port and starboard for the sailors are
signals as for others left and right.
But red and green for drivers of a car
draw their attention only by their light.

The choice of red and green, however,
points to their contrast which says either or,
mistaking left for right is never clever,
not stopping at a red light you deplore.

Nature, you see, puts red and green together
and other colours, which you wouldn't dare.
It never once must wonder whether
sailors or drivers are supposed to care.

## Single

A single coloured flower here stands out
as if it didn't need its own green leaves.
You know it has, but this is all about
distributing seeds. Next year no single grieves.

People who stay single can as well
propagate ideas that take their seed
in kindred minds and with time swell
to bear the fruit that other people need.

No one is quite alone here, by the way.
We are surrounded by so many others.
But individuals are prone to say
that their own life 's what really bothers.

# Lightcatcher

One spot of light can be enough
to detect a tiny flower.
Its life in the wilderness is tough
to resist stronger plants or shower.

Who catches the light has already won:
the plants can prosper and grow,
whereas those that permanently shun
the limelight eventually slow.

The light of public attention, however,
is a danger all of its own.
To avoid it seems to be awfully clever,
you're freer when you are unknown.

# Wallflowers

Wallflowers can be beautiful, you see,
although they often are not recognized,
as they are shy to show their quality
and wilt before it's truly realized.

So when a person tries to fade away,
and blend in crowds not really to be seen,
tell them to take courage and to stay
and show that they are well adept and keen.

For everybody has an inborn gift
that has to be discovered, it is true,
but with some effort they can always try and lift
it from the unknown, show what they can do.

**Not planted but growing**

In smallest crevices you see
pretty flowers blooming
and wonder just how it can be
that even stones are rooming.

They seem to offer quite enough
for seeds to grow and spread
which are astonishingly tough,
this makes caretakers mad.

For once they settle in the ground
the plants do multiply
and are between more stones then found
into whose gaps they pry.

## Out of place

These leaves look somehow out of place:
an alien in the lake,
or just a stand-alone nutcase
which poses for its sake?

So what if it grew unaware
of where it would unfold?
As with the child for who you care,
who defies what they're told.

The plants can't really choose their stand
but animals and man
can use their feet, sometimes their hand,
accomplish what they can.

Wherever they come out to be,
above the surface they are free.

## As green as possible

Some greens are greener than the green we know.
They shine so clear that you avert your eyes.
It is a wonder nature 's keen to show,
whose brilliancy surpasses human tries.

Soft to the touch the leaves greet us in spring,
already they succeed to catch the sun,
transform its energy to make a useful thing
that as sugar any foodchain has begun.

This practical perspective set aside
the beech tree is a favourite in my place.
It opens hearts and eyes in spring just wide
as its reflection can be seen on our face.

# Those spring greens

**Norbert Rath**

In spring the trees push different greens
to greet the warmth that settles
on lakes and ground and softly leans
on trees and bush and nettles.

The frogs which feel their life in spring
croak their concert competition,
and all the birds that love to sing
do so from top position.

Deep down in creatures and in us
the spring of life does burst,
and everybody's in a fuss
because we feel life's thirst.

## The biggest trees can't hide the sun

**Norbert Rath**

Sometimes you think you take a thumb
and hide the sun completely.
But then, of course, you are not dumb
and know it won't work neatly.

The sun just looks so small that you
believe you're in control
until the sun does barbecue
our whole world as its toll.

Even the highest trees could not
withstand the glaring power
and all the life would burn, then rot,
man, animals and flower.

51

## Evening light

The sun goes down and makes the shadows longer
until only the trees are bathed in light.
Back in the day the sunrays were much stronger,
temperatures drop now, causing sheer delight.

A slight breeze waves the evening air and pushes
the grass so that it calmly sways its seeds.
The leaves start trembling slightly on the bushes
and trees, a sound as if a gentle voice soft reads.

The evening song of birds chatters good-bye
to the hot day when life was in full swing.
And when the woods in darker shadows lie
with luck a single nightingale begins to sing.

# Go to sleep

Norbert Rath

Go to sleep - the sun is on its way
when some old clouds dip orange in the sky.
Before they carry rain they now turn grey
and wait until the day that makes them cry.

The woods lose every light to darkness spreading
when night sounds whisper in the room around.
Animals of the night now leave their bedding
to find new prey either by smell or by a sound.

The day leaves silently and says good-byes
to all the hustles that so need the light,
and when I finally give in and close my eyes
I welcome sleep to live dreams in the night.

Everybody knows

that once is not enough

except in some cases.


This is not the case here:

reading a poem once

is not enough,

but then

you don't have to read more than one

per day.


**Enjoy!**

www.ingramcontent.com/pod-product-compliance
Lightning Source LLC
Chambersburg PA
CBHW050820290526
45792CB00001B/193